THE POWERFUL MINDSET FOR SUCCESS

Personal Development Goals for Thriving Humans

NORA U.I

Contents

INTRODUCTION

Personal growth is a potent process that can result in profound, beneficial, and long-lasting changes in how we view the world and ourselves. You can realize your potential, actualize your potential, and accomplish your goals with personal development.

Three main areas are benefited by personal development:

1. Awareness of oneself. Self-awareness is the first step towards personal development. Realizing your genuine self is the first step on the discovery path, allowing you to reach your full potential.

2. Establishes Direction. A new belief that you can accomplish your goals and be in a better position to make decisions about your future will be created as a result of the process of getting more in tune with who you are and what you want.

3. Action and motivation. Personal development abilities can assist you in maintaining your attention and motivation once a decision has been made to pursue your objectives.

The goal of personal growth or development is as easy as taking a moment to reflect and resolve to be greater. Self-help books, training courses, meditation, private journals, poetry, and art are all part of the development process.

According to one definition of personal development,

Personal development is the deliberate pursuit of personal improvement through increased self-awareness, knowledge, and competence.

Activities that promote consciousness and identity, foster talent and potential, create human capital and facilitate employability, improve quality of life, and help realize hopes and aspirations are all considered to be part of personal development.

Personal growth is a process that lasts a lifetime. It's a crucial technique for encouraging you to pause, reflect on your goals in life, evaluate your talents and attributes, and set objectives in order to realize and maximize your potential.

The idea goes beyond self-help and encompasses official and informal activities for training people to fill a variety of positions, such as teachers, mentors, guides, counselors, managers, and life coaches.

The approaches, programs, tools, techniques, and assessment systems that support human growth at the individual level in organizations are referred to as personal development in the context of institutions.

Strengthening self-awareness

Enhancing or regaining identity and self-worth

Enhancing abilities or skills

Raising wealth

Spiritual growth

Finding or enhancing potential

Building human capital or employability

Improving one's lifestyle or quality of life

Enhancing health

Achieving objectives

Starting a life venture or achieving personal autonomy

The creation and implementation of personal development plans

Enhancing social skills

The idea encompasses more than just self-improvement or self-help; it also includes the growth of others. This may be accomplished through positions such as teacher or mentor, either through a personal competency (such the capability of some managers to develop the potential of staff) or a professional service (such as providing training, assessment or coaching).

Personal development is more than just growing oneself and others; it is a subject of study and practice. Its scope of practice covers strategies, instruments, systems of assessment, learning programs, and ways for personal growth. Personal development is a growing area of study that is being covered by academic publications, reviews of higher education, journals of management, and business literature.

If one wants to determine whether a change has actually taken place, a framework is necessary for any type of development, whether it be economic, political, biological, organizational, or personal. When it comes to personal growth, the individual frequently serves as the main arbiter of improvement; nonetheless, objective improvement must be validated through evaluation using accepted standards.

Goals or benchmarks that specify end points, plans or tactics for achieving goals, measurements and assessments of progress, levels or stages that specify turning points in a development path, and a feedback system to track changes are all possible components of personal development frameworks.

CHAPTER 1

Frameworks for personal development

Those could be objectives or standards that specify:

The focal points

Strategies

Goal-achieving plans

Measurement

Evaluation of progress

Milestones in a development route are defined by levels or stages.

A feedback mechanism that notifies users of changes

Take a look at our extensive selection of award-winning personal development courses, training, and coaching packages if you're ready to grow personally and professionally.

Why is it vital to pursue personal growth?

Personal development has countless advantages. You can achieve your goals and overcome obstacles with its assistance. The secret to obtaining personal success is understanding how to make plans and create goals.

Personal development is a broad issue, and when people use the term, it can refer to a variety of things, from improving one's quality of life to moving one's job to the next level.

I really believe that we all need to comprehend the concept of personal growth because life itself is a process of ongoing learning, despite the fact that the majority of people have no idea what it exactly is and have no clear plan for it.

Therefore, if you ignore them or don't deliberately establish plans for development, you might wake up one day and realize that you're truly leading a life you don't enjoy, at which point it might be too late to make changes.

This justifies the significance of personal development. You want to make sure you are living a life that is worthwhile because you only get to live once.

If you want to live on your own terms and circumstances, you don't want to wake up at 65 and realize you've squandered decades living someone else's life.

The following list outlines the top 7 reasons why personal growth is crucial, particularly if you want to have a more fruitful, meaningful, and successful life:

1. Widens your viewpoint

First, via ongoing learning, personal development broadens your perspective. Whether you like it or not, change is a constant. And you will eventually lose your job if you keep working on the same thing or refuse to get better.

Additionally, growth can only occur when you step outside of your comfort zone. You will continue to get what you have always gotten if you act in the same way.

For instance, you need to change your behavior if you want to have a better life, make more money, or get healthier. To accomplish your goals, you must create a strategy and make the commitment to follow it through.

But awareness is necessary first. You become conscious that you need to change when you realize something in your life is not working, such as the fact that you are not working at a job you love or that your health is failing.

Additionally, in order to spread awareness, you must have a more positive outlook on your potential.

For instance, when you associate with wealthy people who have achieved far greater financial success than you, you begin to realize that you are capable of more. And when that occurs, your desire to accomplish more will be sparked.

Personal growth is significant since it broadens your viewpoint. The better you can be and do in life, the more you can read, learn, and network.

Therefore, when you start the process of bettering yourself, your perspective instantly broadens so that you can lead a better life.

2. Strengthens your mental fortitude

Yes, self-improvement strengthens your mind.

Knowing yourself is true wisdom; knowing others is intellect. The actual source of power is within; controlling others is strength.

You improve at whatever you do when you have a greater understanding of yourself, including your talents and flaws.

Knowing your strengths and areas for development helps you become a better person.

Then, you can become stronger by assembling a team that is better and more capable of achieving greater objectives.

Additionally, if you have a greater understanding of who you are, you can spend more time and money developing the skills that set you apart from the competition. You excel in your particular field. And this is the time when amazing things will occur.

3. Increases self-assurance

If you want to accomplish your goals and have a successful life, confidence is crucial. Because they don't believe they can succeed, people who lack confidence frequently put off or abandon their goals.

You will discover more after you start your road to bettering yourself. Your confidence will increase when you achieve your goals, pick up new talents, and get better at what you do. Being confident becomes second nature to you.

You can become more assured about a subject about which you lack confidence by learning more about it.

Being confident ultimately comes down to preparation. You will feel confident since you are fully prepared when you are facing a challenge.

As a result, personal development helps you become more assured in your abilities.

4. Makes you tenacious

Grit is one of the traits that most accurately predicts success, not IQ, social skills, or even physical appearance. Grit is perseverance and enthusiasm. You can also become more tenacious by engaging in personal growth. In other words, you grow more resilient and capable of greater achievement as you continually strive to develop yourself in all facets of life.

You'll develop a stronger interest for a subject as you learn more about it. How much do you know about tennis, really?

If you have a strong interest in tennis, you probably know a lot about the sport, including the top players, the different serves, the points, etc. If tennis isn't your passion, you probably won't bother learning more about it.

Therefore, knowledge and desire complement one another. A subject might pique your interest when you learn more about it. You will learn more about something if you are passionate about it. A two-way cycle exists.

This indicates that you should devote yourself to personal growth if you want to be more successful and lead a more satisfying life. Learn everything you can because as you grow as a person, grit will follow.

5. Offers a sense of orientation

You become more aware of what you want out of life when you work on improving yourself. Additionally, this provides you a sense of purpose that may influence your decision-making in other areas of your life.

Because they lack a clear life direction, the majority of individuals are not living their dreams and are content with living mediocre lives. They go where others go because they are following the herd. They are stranded.

However, you will find what you really desire if you work on developing yourself, study, learn, and make a commitment to doing so.

Your life goals are very obvious to you. Making decisions becomes simpler, and you stop wasting time (and life) on things that don't actually matter.

You see, when your goals are clear, you know what to do and may take use of Pareto's 80/20 Rule to increase your effectiveness. But if you don't know what you want to get out of life, you'll try everything and end up feeling aimless.

You will have a deeper understanding of yourself as you seek to enhance yourself. You will know what you want out of life after you have a deeper understanding of yourself.

You can now clearly see where you wish to go as a result.

The foundation of your success is having a clear idea of what you want to accomplish. Work on bettering yourself if you are still unsure of what you want from life. Make strategies to improve your life and commit to growing personally.

6. Increases concentration and productivity

Clarity improves as a result of personal development, as we have already mentioned. Additionally, you can prioritize your priorities once your objectives are clear.

You are able to work more effectively since it improves your concentrate.

What presents the largest challenge to maintaining focus? Distraction. You can never perform excellent work if you are continually sidetracked. Your ability to concentrate and give your all will prevent you from performing at your best at work, which will reduce your effectiveness.

You become more concentrated when you are dedicated to your personal development. You are certain that you can accomplish your goals because you are clear about them, your priorities, and what you desire. As a result, you become more productive and focused.

Additionally, you won't feel as much strain and tension while you are concentrated. Only when you're feeling overburdened will you feel pressure and tension. However, you will be able to clearly see the big picture when you are concentrated.

And once more, this demonstrates the significance of personal development and the need for a self-improvement strategy.

7. Increases your success

Do I need to elaborate further? After making the decision to pursue personal development and starting your journey, you will see that you are improving and moving closer to having a better life every day.

You won't get there right away, and it might take some time, but if you're committed to moving forward, you will.

Many people lack commitment to personal growth. They are unwilling to read. They are unwilling to learn. They also have no desire to become better people. They are largely trapped in life as a result of this.

They continue to live in this manner despite having no notion what they desire. Instead of spending time making plans for their lives and deciding what they want, they prefer to watch TV and make plans for their weekends.

Do not behave in a common manner.

So, make a commitment to your personal growth. Make reading, learning something new, and continually bettering oneself a daily habit.

CHAPTER TWO

Skills for Personal Development

Personal characteristics, personality traits, innate social cues, and communication skills are examples of personal development skills. Self-improvement, which focuses on enhancing your knowledge, skills, and self-awareness to achieve your personal goals, is a necessary component of developing these skills.

How can I strengthen my abilities in personal development?

1. Discover something fresh

Your personal development abilities can be enhanced by picking up a new pastime, enrolling in a course, reading a book, or educating oneself on a subject. Your mind and senses will alter as a result, which will help you develop your skills.

2. Take up Volunteering

Active service troops, their families, retirees, veterans, and civilians have the chance to interact with their installation and neighborhood resources through volunteering. Participating in volunteer work can help you improve your interpersonal, managerial, organizational, and public speaking abilities on a personal and professional level.

Ways to enhance one's personal development

You'll be on the correct track to gaining the crucial personal development skills if you can figure out how to comprehend how your behaviors, emotions, and motives operate. Joining one of our coaching packages or courses from the list above is a surefire way to start your personal development journey.

There are seven techniques to improve your personal growth abilities.

There is no better approach to better oneself and achieve one's goals than to enhance one's personal development abilities.

Personal development is a constant process that involves evaluating and revising your objectives, principles, and behaviors before developing the abilities and traits required to achieve them.

Even the most shy individuals may find this procedure intimidating and laborious, yet it can significantly improve one's personal and professional lives by helping them sort through the "noise" that holds them back from realizing their potential.

The following are some of the most crucial personal development abilities that anyone can pick up to increase their capability and confidence.

1. Face and conquer your fears

Fear is the dream-killer since it might keep you from changing and moving closer to your objectives. The more time you spend being overcome by dread, the more it will hinder your progress and bring you down.

Step away from your comfort zone. Take a speech class or join a debate group if you feel uncomfortable speaking in front of groups of people. Find a mentor who can help you make wise judgments if you're afraid to take chances.

As terrifying as it may sound, if you are put in a scenario that will force you to face and overcome your fears, you are more likely to learn and feel confident in yourself.

2. Increase the range of your reading.

One of the finest methods to increase one's vocabulary and knowledge is to read. Additionally, it aids in informational maintenance. One can learn more about themselves and their place in the world by reading more books.

By presenting you with novel circumstances, it can also serve to stimulate your mind and enhance your capacity for critical thought. To do this, make an effort to read one book or at least one article that is informative or inspirational every day.

3. Develop a new talent or skill

Learning a new ability or skill can be very advantageous for you because it can increase your potential by broadening your skill set. This can broaden your perspective and provide you the tools you need to meet new difficulties.

You can either enroll in classes relevant to your line of work, like programming or creative writing, to give yourself an edge. In addition, you can enroll in courses in subjects unrelated to your line of work, such first aid or entrepreneurship. Even while these abilities might not add much to your profession, they can still be useful in other contexts.

4. Request input from people on your work.

The first meal of excellent leaders and high-performing teams is feedback. You can identify the areas where you can improve by getting an outside, unbiased opinion of your work.

Receiving criticism enables you to analyze your behavior and make improvements, which helps you avoid repeating the same mistakes. Asking for feedback on a current project or accomplishment from a relative, friend, coworker, or management might help one identify areas for improvement.

5. Pay attention to others and take notes.

You can develop yourself by learning from a mentor or a coworker whose behavior and objectives motivate you to work harder. Choose the traits you admire in them, and strive to embody those traits in yourself.

Talking to a mentor is another way to accomplish this. They might be your manager, a lecturer, somebody you look up to, or a mentor for your career or personal development. Finding strategies to improve your self-development abilities might be made easier by having someone you can look up to and learn from.

6. Widen your contact base

People are social beings. These social networks are seen as crucial for one's professional success because of the influence our communities have on us throughout our lives.

You can pick up new concepts by interacting with a variety of coworkers. You get the chance to learn how to interact and work with various personality types.

By joining trade associations and other organizations with similar interests, one might broaden their network and meet people who may be useful to them in the future.

7. Journal and practice meditation

Self-awareness is a crucial personal growth ability, and journaling and meditation are the greatest ways to cultivate it.

You can reflect on recent events, choices, and interactions by journaling. After that, you may use this to gauge how well you're doing in relation to your objectives and adjust as needed in light of your reflections.

In the interim, meditation can assist you in focusing on your personal growth in a healthy, upbeat, and relaxed manner. It can help you become more attentive and clear-headed, as well as less stressed out. Setting aside time to meditate or write in a journal might help you unwind and concentrate.

How to improve your personal growth abilities

Personal development skills are traits and prowess that can aid in your professional and personal growth, allowing you to reach your full potential.

The best course of action for you is to carefully consider which abilities you wish to acquire. Make sure that these qualities will help you advance in your career or sector while also allowing you to develop as a person.

What distinguishes personal growth from self-development?

The purpose of personal growth is to acquire new abilities and methods for achieving objectives in life. Self-development focuses on making the things in your life that are already good.

CHAPTER THREE

Aims for one's own development

A clear plan for personal development and the identification of growth areas can have a big impact on your career. These personal development objectives may assist you in broadening your knowledge, enhancing your skills, or improving your performance in your position.

Personal development objectives are targets you create to enhance your personality, competencies, and skills. In order to achieve these goals and reach your full potential, you must first evaluate yourself and determine your areas of improvement. Make a strategy with specific steps in order to begin your personal development. These actions will help you gauge your progress and maintain focus on your goal.

Advantages of setting professional growth objectives

Goals for personal growth are crucial since they can result in professional advancement. Setting career-related personal development objectives has the following advantages:

-Unambiguous sense of orientation

You may complete projects with a strong sense of direction and improved focus when you have clearly defined goals. A list of priorities can help you decide when to start each activity, how much time to spend on it, and how frequently to delegate it. Because you are aware of how important the work you need to complete is, personal development goals help you put distractions out of your life.

-An enhanced work ethic

You are more likely to tackle activities with dedication if you have goals for yourself. Your hope for accomplishing those objectives should be a strong drive behind every task you take on.

-Better interpersonal ties at work

A dedication to personal growth can frequently assist you in preserving productive interactions with your coworkers. The benefit of strong relationships can become obvious as you develop personally, and you might end up serving as an example for other workers.

-An increase in output

Personal growth will ultimately boost your productivity at work. As you achieve each of your objectives, anticipate higher effectiveness, more production, and improved outcomes.

How to set work-related personal development objectives

Follow these steps to start setting and accomplishing career-related personal development objectives:

1. Establish a goal

To determine your personal growth objectives, first evaluate your performance and desires. Create a clear picture of what you want to be or where you want to be in the future by using these objectives or areas for progress. This vision should be quantifiable, actionable, practical, and time-bound, just like your goals should be. Think about your reasons for having this vision and make careful note of them.

2. Create a strategy

Making a plan to realize your vision is the next stage. Decide which areas you need to improve in order to reach your goal, then start articulating goals to do so. Separate each objective into achievable, little stages.

Do not forget that learning is a process of personal development. Before continuing, take the time to determine your preferred method of learning in order to choose the most suitable improvement strategy for each objective.

3. Monitor your development

As you work toward your goals, keep track of your progress. Keep track of the adjustments you make and how they affect your career. You'll learn the best practices as you go along and get closer to your objectives.

Use software tools or a notebook planner to regularly track your progress. A vision board is a visual tool that presents your goal as the central idea and surrounds it with the smaller goals you need to accomplish to realize your vision. You can also decide to use this strategy. You can include images and photos of your plans and place the board in a spot where you will see it daily.

4. Review your plan regularly

It is important to return to your plan periodically to determine if the path you are on is worthwhile. Consider what you have learned so far and decide if your plan is still relevant. Depending on your progress, you can adjust your timelines and create space to include new personal development goals.

Examples of personal development goals for work

There are many goals you could set to begin a personal development plan. Consider choosing one of these common personal development goals:

-Improve your time management

To make the best use of your time in the workplace, allocate a timeline to every task and follow it diligently. Time management skills can increase your productivity and efficiency.

-Develop emotional intelligence

Emotional intelligence describes your control over your emotions and your level of empathy. Developing this skill can make you a better communicator with your colleagues. In addition, it can help you to resolve workplace conflicts—a useful trait for leaders and managers.

-Cultivate resilience

A resilient individual moves on from difficult situations quickly. Resilience can be a great fit as a personal development goal because it keeps you moving forward regardless of denials, rejections and pushback. With resilience, you will stay focused on your tasks until you achieve them. Resilience is a major attribute of problem-solvers.

-Listen actively

An active listener assimilates what they have heard and considers that information carefully before providing a response or taking any action. Active listening is an essential communication skill, so this is a helpful goal if you want to become a better communicator. It can also help you build trust with your coworkers.

-Develop a growth mindset

A growth mindset is a way of thinking that upholds hard work and dedication as the keys to success and improvement. With it, you are resilient and see failures as learning opportunities. When you challenge yourself this way, you can achieve results in the workplace. Moreover, a growth mindset will improve the way you set goals for yourself, tracking learnings as well as performance.

-Develop a reading habit

Reading more is a great personal development goal because it has many benefits, including that it is a means of education. There are books on all subjects, including areas related to professional fields. Invest in them and create a reading schedule for yourself. Furthermore, reading is a means of opening yourself to the experiences of others. This gives you multiple perspectives on the world and informs the decisions you make. Altogether, this improves your competence in the workplace.

-Learn new things

Committing to learning new things is a key step in personal development. While reading is one method, you can also perform research, sign up for courses or take advantage of online learning, such as massive open online courses (MOOCs). Most of the courses offered through these learning platforms offer a certificate that you can add to your resume to showcase your new competencies.

-Improve your public speaking skills

A good public speaker is clear, confident and engaging. Public speaking is important to the workplace because you may have to address your team in a briefing, deliver a presentation to the board or pitch to prospective clients. You can join an organization or take a class to advance your public speaking skills.

-Meet new people

Making new business contacts is a great way to build a network and expand the opportunities available to you in your industry. Creating new relationships can also result in opportunities for you to share your ideas with others and learn from them.

CHAPTER FOUR

Identifying your skills and passions

That's not actually how passion operates. It is necessary to identify your passions before you can follow them. To find the job that appeals to your enthusiasm, you'll probably need to put in many days of work in a variety of contexts.

Here are some tips on how to identify your passion and pursue it so that you can lead a more fulfilling life.

There are times when our passions are things we would love to do for a living. Sometimes what we really want is what we think we want. Being passionate about our work is different from being eager or enthusiastic about it.

Understanding the difference between passions and basic beliefs is crucial. Everyone has a unique set of guiding principles that determine how they behave and how they perceive their jobs and workplaces. Discipline, persistence, playfulness, learning, excellence, and resilience are examples of strong core values.

Finding and pursuing your hobbies is a key factor in determining the degree of success you're going to have, both professionally and personally, according to researchers and vocational experts.

The intriguing thing about following your passions is that you'll always want to accomplish more of what you care about on an intellectual and emotional level. This implies that achieving advancement in your profession and personal development are directly related to finding and nurturing your passions. However, it isn't always as simple as figuring out how to make money from what you enjoy doing in your free time. Finding the threads of passion that link a hobby or interest to a vocation or profession frequently requires using your imagination.

You can follow these 10 steps to discover your passion:

Make a vision statement for yourself.

Choose your values.

Discover your true north.

Make a list of your favorite activities.

Consider what you don't like.

Recognize your accomplishments and strengths.

Maintain a journal.

Adopt a mindfulness routine

Consult a coach for advice.

Make friends with others who share your passions.

Let's examine each of these actions in detail.

Finding your passion

On a more personal level, happiness and contentment are frequently correlated with discovering your passion.

For this reason, if you want to live a fulfilling life, you must discover your passion. However, you might be thinking, "How can I discover my passion?"

Check out these detailed instructions on how to begin discovering your passion. Waiting will only make it take longer.

It takes trying out several jobs and other activities to find and expose your passions. It is uncommon to be passionate about something we have little knowledge of. To fall in love with a pursuit, you must first have some comprehension of it, become familiar with its difficulties and difficulties, or to desire to work on it daily.

Remember that discovering your passions is a process that takes time and doesn't happen all at once. Your interests may shift over your life. That's alright.

1. Draft a vision statement for oneself.

Your goals for your personal and professional life are outlined in your personal vision statement.

It functions a lot like a compass to show direction. It directs you anytime significant choices must be made. Your personal vision statement might help you discover your genuine passions after it is written.

2. Determine your values

Your personal values are the things that you hold dear to guide how you live and operate. Your own objectives and ambitions are determined by your values. And they frequently serve as a gauge of whether or not your life and career path are going in the direction you intended.

3. Discover your true north.

Finding your true north is a concept that is closely related to becoming more aware of your basic principles. It is about learning what drives you. What motivation or objective drives you? What do you do that makes you feel fulfilled, in the moment, and as though you are fulfilling your purpose?

What some people refer to as realizing who you truly are, your authentic or full self, is finding your true north. Your values, convictions, and feeling of purpose come together to form your true north.

And holding compass near beach how to find your passion

You'll be that much closer to leading a fulfilled life that is motivated by your passions once you become aware of your true north.

4. Compile a list of your favorite activities.

In the words of Socrates, "Man know yourself." He is stressing the value of individuals understanding themselves before asserting (or attempting to assert) their knowledge of anything else.

To obtain this self-knowledge, make a list of your favorite activities. Developing self-awareness is a crucial step in identifying your passions.

5. Evaluate the things you dislike.

Realizing what you enjoy doing and what you love to accomplish is crucial. However, it's equally crucial to evaluate the things you detest. You'll have a better idea of the characteristics that define you if you can identify what you don't love.

6. Recognize your accomplishments and strengths

Recognize your accomplishments and strengths in order to find your genuine self. People frequently discover that their biggest personal assets are the things that naturally come to them. Once you know this, you'll have even more motivation to work hard and complete more difficult tasks.

7. Try keeping a journal.

The act of journaling may seem unrelated to discovering and pursuing our passions to the inexperienced ear. But the truth is that keeping a journal enables us to monitor our development as people.

Keeping a journal gives us a place to explore our own passions. Without interference from others' judgments or restricting views, we can identify our areas of passion.

8. Adopt a mindfulness routine.

Living in the present requires practicing mindfulness. It also entails accepting wellness and being mindful of all of your feelings and experiences, without passing judgment or engaging in excessive analysis or interpretation.

We all already know what we are passionate about, according to mindfulness. Just to make conscious contact with the knowledge, we need a "vehicle."

Adopting a mindfulness practice enables us to connect with our inner compass more deeply. The best method to enable our actual emotions and desires to surface in our conscious brains is frequently in this manner.

9. Consult a coach for advice.

A coach can be a useful tool while trying to discover your passion.

For instance, a career coach has received training in assisting individuals in discovering their life's and career passions. We can free ourselves from the weight of outside pressure by working with career coaches.

10. Surround yourself with those who share your interests.

To successfully surround oneself with people who share your passions, there is simply one secret. Learn what motivates, reassures, and inspires you. You'll know you've met someone when you see such attributes in them—passions that are comparable to your own.

What distinguishes hobbies from passions?

A hobby is something you love doing in your spare time and for enjoyment. A passion is something that you always have within of you. Something you feel motivated to continue doing even in the absence of outside rewards like pay or praise. Some people's calling in life is a career in medicine. Like political history, it is an academic subject for some. Others may associate it with a certain process or activity, such as sculpting or programming.

The possibility exists, nonetheless, for a new talent or interest to develop into a passion.

Let's examine some instances of passions as opposed to hobbies:

Volunteering to conserve sea turtles is preferable to maintaining a marine aquarium for the purpose of home decoration.

Instead of signing up for a gym companion in your leisure time, consider exercising to get and keep your body in top shape.

Instead of collecting expensive jewelry as a pastime, live your creativity by mastering the art of jewelry-making.

None of this implies that you shouldn't engage in pastimes you enjoy. Hobbies give us a productive outlet for our creativity and a space to dabble with ideas while recharging our mental and physical health.

How Inner Work

The spiritual and psychological activity of deeply exploring your inner self is called Inner Work. All the while pursuing self-knowledge, enlightenment, and even emotional recovery.

In essence, Inner Work introduces people to their own inner worlds. It entails locating our own compass for gazing ahead. Looking inward rather than letting the outside world influence you is what Inner Work entails. In this manner, we are able to spot fresh chances for the fantastic things we are passionate about.

Journaling (as described above), reading, or meditation are all examples of Inner Work. In the end, it comes down to working hard to investigate and comprehend your inner experiences in order to achieve more clarity, purpose, and passion.

What should I do now that I've discovered my passion?

But what happens when you've discovered your passion? What should you do next now that you are aware of your passions? What follows is what?

Always take some sort of action after discovering your passion. You'll be able to keep track of your interests in this way. Should put this knowledge into practice in order to live a happy and fulfilling life.

From a professional perspective, take into account the following:

Take a look at the possibilities. After discovering your passion, it's important to take advantage of the available job prospects. With your newly acquired knowledge, you'll be far more prepared to recognize possibilities and convert them into genuine value.

Evaluate the likelihood of pursuing your passions. It is a fact that not every passion will translate into success in the career, whether it be financially or personally. Because of this, it's crucial to conduct a viability analysis before diving in and attempting to create a living from the activities you find most fulfilling.

Find the essential elements of your passion that translate into career opportunities, such as solving puzzles or solving mysteries. Alternately, look for new interests inside your line of work.

Do it the proper way if you want to quit your job and follow your passion. This is a crucial one. Making a mental note of what you want from your ideal career is one step that needs to be taken in advance. Next, make a comparison between your present position and your dream profession, have a strategy in place, and finally construct the bridge to close the gap.

To assist you, ask a coach for advice. Accepting that there may be people out there who are more knowledgeable than you about a subject is one of the best ways to advance in life. Making your passions into a rewarding profession requires consulting with a career coach.

Also, bear the following in mind regarding your personal interests:

Make your enthusiasm a routine. Take steps to incorporate your passions into your daily life now that you have identified them. You'll want to spend your days doing the things you enjoy, so this will be simple to accomplish. Your life can change for the better if you develop good habits.

Make time for your passions by using time management. Keep in mind that pursuing a hobby is much more than just killing time. This implies that you'll occasionally need to intentionally carve out time to do the activities you enjoy. Keep track of the time you have for your passions by using time management strategies like time blocking.

Discover your passions to live a happy life.

Bottom line: Knowing and doing what you truly enjoy is the key to discovering your passion and leading a successful life.

There are many benefits to spending the time and energy necessary to identify your passions, as well as for stepping outside of your comfort zone to put your newly acquired knowledge into practice.

CHAPTER FIVE

How to formulate a plan of action

Do you intend to realize your vision? What's your best strategy for avoiding difficulties and obstacles along the way? A strong plan of action. In order to build an action plan, follow the six stages we have given. Use the editable templates below to begin planning as soon as you've become familiar with them.

What is a plan of action?

An action plan is a list of the steps or duties you must carry out in order to accomplish the objectives you have set.

It aids in enhancing teamwork planning and is a crucial step in the process of strategic planning. Action plans can be used by people to design a strategy for achieving their own personal goals in addition to project management.

An action plan's elements include.

A clear statement of the objective that must be accomplished

Tasks or steps that must be taken to accomplish the goal

Who will be responsible for performing each task?

When will these projects be finished? (Deadlines and milestones)

Requisite materials for finishing the tasks

Measures for assessing progress

The beautiful thing about having everything in one place is that it makes it simpler to monitor progress and organize things well.

A plan of action is a living document. You will need to examine and make changes to meet the most recent needs as your organization expands and the environment changes.

Why You Need a Plan of Action

Businesses occasionally don't take enough time to create an action plan before launching a project, which typically results in failure. If you didn't know, planning to fail is the same as not planning at all.

You may prepare for upcoming challenges and stay on track by planning. Additionally, you can increase productivity and maintain concentration with a solid action plan.

Following are some advantages of an action plan you should be aware of:

It provides you with a definite path. You will know exactly what to accomplish because an action plan outlines all of the steps that must be taken and the due dates for each one.

Your motivation and commitment to the project will increase if your goals are documented and laid out in detail.

You can monitor your advancement toward your objective with an action plan.

Your action plan will help you prioritize your tasks based on effort and impact because you are outlining all the steps you need to do.

Utilize action plans to your advantage when working. Utilize cordately to stay organized and keep track of all your tasks and objectives in one location.

Make a plan of action

Writing an Action Plan

Making an action plan seems to be a fairly simple process. To make the most of it, though, there are a few crucial procedures you must carefully follow. Here are six simple actions that can help you build an action plan.

Step 1 is to specify your final aim.

You are setting yourself up for failure if you are unclear about what you want to do and achieve.

Considering a fresh endeavor? Set your current location and desired location first.

Resolving a dilemma? Prioritize the remedies after analyzing the problem and considering all of the potential ones.

Next, jot out your objective. Run your goal by the SMART criteria before moving on to the next phase. Alternatively, ensure that it is Specific, well defined, and Measurable - incorporate quantifiable metrics to monitor development Realistic and doable given the time, money, resources, experience, etc. you have Relevant and in line with your other objectives.

Timely - includes a deadline

To make the process simpler, use this spreadsheet for SMART goals. Give it to others so you may get their feedback as well.

Step 2: Compile a list of the necessary steps.

The aim is obvious. What precisely must you do to achieve it?

Make a preliminary outline of the tasks that must be completed, together with their due dates and assignees.

It's crucial that you guarantee that everyone in the team gets access to the document and is active in the process. Everyone will be aware of their obligations and tasks in the project as a result.

Make certain that each task is specific and doable. If you encounter more difficult or complicated jobs, divide them into smaller, more manageable chunks.

Step 3: Set task priorities and deadlines.

It's time to rearrange the list by giving the tasks higher priority. You might need to give some stages more priority because they might be obstructing other sub-processes.

Make sure to include timelines and that they are reasonable. Before setting deadlines, speak with the person in charge of carrying it out to determine their capacity

Step 4: Establish deadlines

Milestones can be thought of as little objectives that serve as a buildup to the main objective. Having milestones gives the team members something to look forward to and keeps them motivated even though the final due date is a long way off.

As you establish milestones, start at the end goal and work your way back. Do not space out the milestones you establish by too much or too little time. Setting milestones two weeks apart is recommended.

Step 5: Determine the resources required

Make sure you have all the tools you'll need on hand to do the chores before you begin your job. You must first devise a strategy to buy them if they are not already in stock.

Step 6: Envision your course of action

The goal of this step is to produce something that can be shared with everyone and understood by everyone at a glance.

Make sure that your action plan properly conveys the components we've already defined, such as tasks, task owners, deadlines, resources, etc., whether it takes the form of a flowchart, Gantt chart, or table.

Step 7: Track, assess, and update

Set aside some time to assess the progress your team has achieved.

On this final action plan, you can highlight your progress by marking items that have been finished as done.

This will also highlight any jobs that are unfinished or behind schedule, in which case you must ascertain the cause and come up with workable alternatives. Afterward, adjust the action plan as necessary.

www.ingramcontent.com/pod-product-compliance
Lightning Source LLC
LaVergne TN
LVHW020526160826
845677LV00015B/3935

* 9 7 9 8 3 5 2 4 3 2 3 4 1 *